This book
belongs to:

Declan Has Fun

Anytime, Anywhere

Coloring Book

Time for fun, anytime, anywhere!

Declan has fun playing with friends.

Declan has fun using his imagination.

Declan has fun shopping.

Declan has fun fishing.

Declan has fun camping.

Declan has fun reading.

Declan has fun skipping.

Declan has fun sharing.

Declan has fun snacking.

Declan has fun cleaning.

Declan has fun watering plants.

Declan has fun riding his bike.

Declan has fun eating an ice cream cone.

Declan has fun throwing leaves.

Declan has fun gardening.

Declan has fun skiing.

Declan has fun building a snowman.

Declan has fun picking a pumpkin.

Declan has fun playing with the dog.

Declan has fun jumping.

Declan has fun turning upside down.

Declan has fun walking with a friend.

Declan has fun hugging his cat.

Declan has fun hiking.

Declan has fun riding.

Declan has fun splashing in puddles.

Declan has fun flying balloons.

How do you
have fun?

66398155R00020